H

Wye Valley

Compiled by
Neil Coates

JARROLD
publishing

 Mapping
sourced from Ordnance
Survey®

Text: Neil Coates
Photography: Neil Coates
Editorial: Ark Creative, Norwich
Design: Ark Creative, Norwich

© Jarrold Publishing 2005

 This product includes mapping data licensed from Ordnance Survey® with the permission of the Controller of Her Majesty's Stationery Office. © Crown Copyright 2005. All rights reserved. Licence number 100017593. Ordnance Survey, the OS symbol and Pathfinder are registered trademarks and Explorer, Landranger and Outdoor Leisure are trademarks of the Ordnance Survey, the national mapping agency of Great Britain.

Jarrold Publishing
ISBN 0-7117-3858-0

First published 2005
by Jarrold Publishing

Printed in Belgium
by Proost NV, Turnhout. 1/05

Jarrold Publishing
Pathfinder Guides, Whitefriars,
Norwich NR3 1TR
email: info@totalwalking.co.uk
www.totalwalking.co.uk

Front cover: The footbridge over the Wye at the Biblins
Previous page: Marcle Ridge

Contents

Keymap 1

SCALE 1:250 000 or 1 INCH to 4 MILES *1CM to 2.5KM*

0   2   4   6   8   10   KILOMETRES   15

0   2   4   6   MILES   8   10

KEYMAP HEIGHTS SHOWN IN FEET

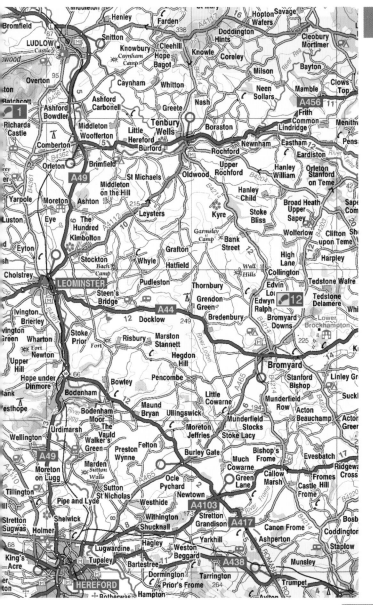

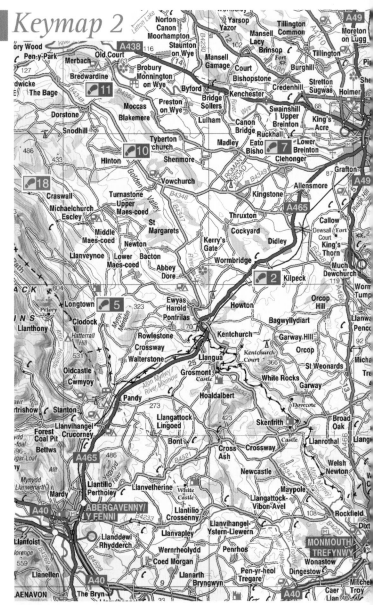

SCALE 1:250 000 or 1 INCH to 4 MILES *1CM to 2.5KM*

| 0 | 2 | 4 | 6 | 8 | 10 | KILOMETRES | | 15 |

| 0 | 2 | 4 | 6 | MILES | 8 | | 10 |

KEYMAP HEIGHTS SHOWN IN FEET

Introduction

With no heavy industry, airports, power stations and little light pollution, Herefordshire is recognised by the Campaign to Protect Rural England (CPRE) as one of only three 'quiet' counties in England. This is where Housman's *Land of Lost Content* still slumbers, a vast morphological bowl of old red sandstone enclosed by uplands including the Black Mountains, Radnor Forest, the Malverns, Forest of Dean and the north Monmouthshire hills.

Within lies a mosaic of black and white villages and medieval farms, ancient churches and ruinous castles threaded together by sinuous byroads. Hop yards and cider orchards provide the raw ingredients for which the county is renowned and the rich red farmland is mirrored in the terracotta hues of the famous Hereford cattle. Low, wooded ridges of limestone and conglomerate pervade a deeply rural landscape dappled by thriving market towns; even the county seat, Hereford, manages to retain much of its rural character.

River Wye and the distant Black Mountains from Coppet Hill

For the serious walker, major recreational trails include Offa's Dyke Path National Trail, Wye Valley Walk, Marches Way, and the Mortimer Trail. Ramblers seeking a short exploration have innumerable choices, from the stunning and remote valleys and hills of the Black Mountains to the lazy backwaters of rivers feeding the Wye and

Severn; between remarkable country chapels and timeless pubs, chocolate box hamlets and half-timbered manors. Red kites soar in the skies whilst otters hunt the waterways and polecats haunt secluded woodlands. Only perhaps at the famous Yat Rock will you be aware of more than a handful of like-minded souls looking for peace, solitude and the land of yore that many wish to rediscover.

Longtown Castle

Castles and forts

There are more fortified sites in the southern Welsh Marches than in any other area of Britain. Iron Age hill forts abound; some obvious, others little visited or disguised beneath forestry plantations.

The most spectacular are those like British Camp, on Herefordshire Beacon in the Malverns, or Croft Ambrey near Leominster – immense earthworks created by generations of labour as places of residence and refuge as much as for purposes of defence and domination. Excavations at Croft Ambrey suggest that it was inhabited for nearly 450 years, whilst British Camp may have been home to as many as 2000 people. Some of the smaller sites were probably simply compounds where livestock and herders could seek protection from wild animals.

It is the remains of the castles built by the Normans and their successors, however, which are amongst the most stunning built features of the Herefordshire landscape. These vary in size and style from the colossal stone edifices such as Goodrich Castle to the myriad mottes that pebbledash the western fringes of the county, scant remains of countless defensive sites that may have been thrown up in little more than a few weeks. The larger ones, the motte-and-bailey castles, are amongst the most evocative architectural elements in the region, tantalising glimpses into the turbulent history of this edge of England.

Many commentators accept that the first Norman castle in England is that above the Golden Valley at Ewyas Harold, established in the 1050s by a Norman nobleman encouraged to settle in these debated border regions by Edward the Confessor, a Saxon king with a Norman upbringing. Whatever the truth of this, the concept of the castle was here to stay; motte-and-bailey sites peppering the countryside as the powerful Norman Earls of the March sought to establish their own fiefdoms and control and tax the Welsh and Saxons whose lands they had usurped.

A hierarchy of castles gradually developed, with major centres of influence boasting substantial stone-built complexes such as those at Wilton, Hay and Wigmore, whilst others developed to help keep the peace and gradually 'Normanize' the area – Almeley, Orcop, Kilpeck and Lingen for example. The result is today's medley of locations; most are jackdaw-haunted ruins but some – Pembridge (near Monmouth) and Croft (near Leominster) – are still lived in. Some are visited along the walks in this book.

Protected landscapes

John Masefield, Poet Laureate in the middle years of the last century, was born in Ledbury. His *Collected Poems* (1946) include verses celebrating the peaceful countryside of the Herefordshire Malverns and the villages and landscapes around this most appealing of market towns, whose church spire is capped by 'a golden vane surveying half the shire'.

The Malvern Hills is an Area of Outstanding Natural Beauty (AONB), a designation that recognises the fragility of the landscape and the need to balance development, agriculture and land use in ways not detrimental to the landscape, whilst acknowledging the needs both of the resident communities and those drawn to the area to enjoy the natural beauty. One of 41 such areas in England and Wales, the designation confers upon the areas a status similar to that of National Parks (the same 1949 Act of Parliament created both classes of landscape). This miniature mountain range, built from some of the oldest rocks in Britain, is further managed and protected by the Malvern Hills Conservators, ensuring that the countryside that so entranced visitors to the thriving spas a century ago, and moved Masefield to verse, is enhanced and retained still.

The Malvern Hills from Edvin Loach

In the south east of Herefordshire is another AONB, the Wye Valley, designated in 1971 in part to help co-ordinate disparate bodies which had for decades worked to conserve the stunning natural and human landscapes that made the area Wordsworth's favourite place outside of the Lake District. From the outskirts of Hereford and the secluded woods and hills of the Woolhope Dome, this AONB encapsulates one of the most spectacular landscapes in lowland Britain, including not only the stunning Wye Gorge but also fringes of the Forest of Dean (designated England's first National Forest Park 70 years ago) and a rich tapestry of timeless villages, farms and manors lost amidst ancient woods and willow-lined streams. Other areas, notably the Monnow and Golden Valleys and the Arcadian landscape of the fringe of the Black Mountains await such statutory protection.

Uniquely in Britain, the River Wye itself is designated as a Site of Special Scientific Interest (SSSI), in recognition of the immense diversity of animals, plants and fish that depend on the cleanliness of the water and the (relative) wildness of the river's course for their well-being. Whilst the Wye's run of salmon, shad and elvers has declined severely in recent decades, they are still of worldwide significance.

The walks in this book offer but the briefest of windows onto this timeless, fascinating county, but it's a taster that, once sampled, will be impossible to forget.

1 *Richard's Castle*

START The Green, Richard's Castle (grid ref: SO 485704)

DISTANCE 2 miles (3.2km)

TIME 1½ hours

PARKING The Green. Turn off the B4361 up the lane beside The Castle Inn in the village centre. Stay with this over a cross lane and pass by The Green Farm. The Green is just beyond, marked by a sign for the castle and church

ROUTE FEATURES Tarred lanes; field paths and farm roads. One gentle ascent; stiles and gates

Richard's Castle parish straddles the Herefordshire/Shropshire border and includes much of that which gives the Marches its distinct character. Grassy commons, wooded knolls and sharp valleys speckled by ancient cottages and manors, secluded villages and remarkable views. This easy walk offers a taster into such heritage, passing one of the country's very first castles and revealing an enviable panorama over the best that rural England can offer.

Put the sublime Church Cottage on your left and walk to the tarred lane. Bear left and walk round the bend. In 150 yds (137m) turn left up a side road, commencing an easy ascent up the flank of Hanway Common. Off to your left you'll soon see some of the castle earthworks beyond renovated buildings. Gaps in the hedgerows offer tantalising glimpses of the ever expanding views that you will be able to enjoy later in the walk.

Ⓐ The lane levels out at a gateway and cattle-grid. Cross this and continue left along this tarred strip across the common. As the lane bends right to climb towards Vallets Farm, keep ahead along a well-defined sheep track across the greensward, roughly parallel to a fence line on your left.

This is part of Hanway Common, one of a string of commons along a high ridge of Aymestry limestone that slices across north

PUBLIC TRANSPORT Buses from Ludlow and Leominster to The Castle Inn, 1 mile (1.6km) from the start

REFRESHMENTS The Castle Inn

PUBLIC TOILETS None

ORDNANCE SURVEY MAPS Explorer 203 (Ludlow)

? *In which year was St Bartholomew's Church abandoned?*

Herefordshire. For over 700 years local commoners have exercised their right to graze animals on these slopes. Farther uphill the trees of Mortimer Forest feather the skyline; this is named in

The Clee Hills from Hanway Common

memory of the Mortimer family, most powerful and feared of the medieval Marcher lords.

Views from here are magnificent. Far ahead, the distinct wall of the Black Mountains rises along the Welsh border whilst off to the left and well beyond the valley of the meandering River Teme, are the Malvern Hills. Looking back, the distinctive Titterstone Clee Hill is topped by a radar dome.

The common gradually narrows to a fine corner and a selection of gates; our route is through the one leading into a hedged track, marked as the route of the Mortimer Trail, a 30-mile recreational footpath between Ludlow and Kington.

Richard's Castle, St Bartholomew's Church

In about 200 yds (183m) take the bridleway waymarked to the left via a metal gate, then keep close to the hedge on your left.

B At the wooded corner go through another gate waymarked with a blue arrow and fork left along the more distinct track that gradually drops into a dingle. Beyond a gate this becomes a pronounced field road, soon reaching a ford and a gnarled oak. Cross the footbridge and continue along the rough lane, sweeping beneath the wooded castle hill.

Just before reaching the barns go through the gate, left, and head half right to another gate beside a cottage. Straight on is The Green, whilst left through a gate gives access to the churchyard of St

It was **Edward the Confessor**, a Saxon king with Norman leanings, who granted land to the Norman nobleman Richard FitzScrob in about AD1050. He built a motte-and-bailey castle – **Richard's Castle** – to help control and defend against the Celtic Welsh in this disputed borderland (or March, hence Marches) and this is incorporated in the overgrown remains visible next to the churchyard. Well before the famous Norman Conquest of 1066, this is one of the earliest castles in England.

Bartholomew's Church. The Norman church, with its distinctive detached bell tower, only has a handful of services each year, but is well maintained by the Churches Conservation Trust. Beyond the churchyard rises the castle mound. There's a fascinating local history board in the upper churchyard.

Kilpeck

START Kilpeck
(grid ref: SO 445305)
DISTANCE 2 miles (3.2km)
TIME 1 hour
PARKING Kilpeck Church
ROUTE FEATURES Easy walking on field paths and back lanes

2

Lost amongst a latticework of narrow country lanes is that classic medieval triumvirate of village life: church, inn and manor. Herefordshire is full of such hidden gems, but here at Kilpeck, the early Norman church is generally regarded as the very finest of its type in Britain. Take ample time to explore this idyllic location before rising very gently to enjoy great views across the rich farmland of western Herefordshire.

At the west side of the church-yard a stile leads to the remains of Kilpeck's castle. King Offa had a defensive site here in the AD780s, but the remains today are 12th century, with a few walls from the keep still standing. To the north east of the motte is the site of an abandoned village. The church itself is on the site of the cell of a Dark Ages monk St Pedic, recorded here around AD650, whilst a Saxon church has left a few stones incorporated into the chancel.

Leave the churchyard and walk ahead with the medieval court house to your left. Some of the stone here came from the old castle. At the junction is The Red Lion pub, a welcoming old village local beside the village green. To the left of the car park is a driveway and cattle-grid. Walk up this and pass immediately right of the half-timbered 'Priory' to climb a stile beyond a lawned area. A further stile leads into a large pasture; here look slightly left for a stile into a strip of trees. At the far side head half left to a gate in line with the white painted cottage on the low ridge ahead.

PUBLIC TRANSPORT Market day buses to Kilpeck from Hereford
REFRESHMENTS Pub in Kilpeck
PUBLIC TOILETS None
ORDNANCE SURVEY MAPS Explorer 189 (Hereford & Ross-on-Wye)

Apart from the modest furnishings and a lick of whitewash inside, little has changed at **Kilpeck's tiny church** since it was built around AD1150. The durable old red sandstone has weathered well, meaning that the fascinating and intricate carvings remain very fresh. The stonemasons allowed their imaginations to run riot – see if you can spot a muzzled bear, pig's head, musicians, a man riding a sheep, rabbits, even stylised crocodiles amongst 80 carved corbel stones around the outside fringe of the church. The south doorway is magnificent.

Ⓐ Turn right along the lane, shortly passing a house and barns.

At the junction, keep left along the 'Dead End' lane and walk a farther 250 yds (228m) to a left bend. On the right here is a finger-posted stile beside a gate. Marvellous views stretch west to the Black Mountains and north to Radnor Forest and the Clee Hills. Climb the stile and aim just left of the woods ahead. Another stile beside a cattle trough leads to a faint field road dropping to the woodland

? *To which saints is Kilpeck Church dedicated?*

Kilpeck Church

Detail of the medieval carving on Kilpeck Church

point where the field widens and head half left to the corner cottage.

B Do not cross the stile here, but turn sharp right to a stile and footbridge in the lower right corner. Trace the field edge over another stile to reach a corner near a cottage. Take the stile beside the gate (not the stile into the garden) and walk left for 70 yds (64m) to a stile into a lane. Turn right; then keep left at the junction to return to the pub. Turn left to the church. ●

corner. Take a stile here and bend right, keeping the woods on your right. Bend left as the woods peel away to find a gate, right, in 100 yds (91m). Take this, walk to the

3 *Midsummer Hill*

This easy walk includes a short climb – but as you're in the midst of the Malvern Hills this is only to be expected! Your reward is one of the most memorable views in Herefordshire; from the ramparts of a hill fort on Hollybush Hill you can see 50 miles on a clear day. The walk also touches the edge of the deer park belonging to Eastnor Castle; the deer here are relatively unfazed by people, so you may be lucky and see some at close quarters.

START Hollybush
(grid ref: SO 758368)
DISTANCE 2½ miles (4km)
TIME 1½ hours
PARKING Eastnor Castle Estate car park, Hollybush, beside A438 2 miles east of Eastnor (free car park open to all – look for a telegraph pole mounted telephone sign, the car park entrance is here)
ROUTE FEATURES Easy walking on lanes; tracks and paths. One short climb

Bizarrely, your route is signposted as the Worcestershire Way (north), although here you're just in Herefordshire; the county line approximately follows the ridge here at the southern end of the Malvern Hills. Follow the tarred lane gently uphill. At a bend, views open out left across the Eastnor estate to the remarkable castle, huddled in a hollow amidst the wooded lower slopes of the Malverns. Simply stay on this lane; once past an isolated cottage it roughens, passes through a

gateway and drops to a junction of tracks beside a tall gate.

The Malverns from Hollybush Hill Fort

PUBLIC TRANSPORT Infrequent summer bus service to Hollybush from Malvern and Ledbury
REFRESHMENTS None en route; all services in Ledbury 4 miles (6.4km)
PUBLIC TOILETS None
ORDNANCE SURVEY MAPS Explorer 190 (Malvern Hills & Bredon Hill)

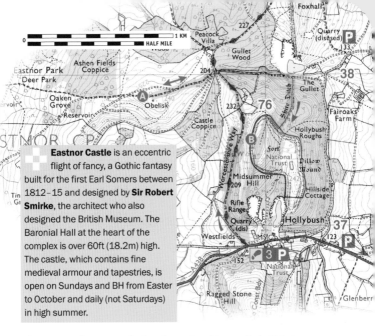

Eastnor Castle is an eccentric flight of fancy, a Gothic fantasy built for the first Earl Somers between 1812–15 and designed by **Sir Robert Smirke**, the architect who also designed the British Museum. The Baronial Hall at the heart of the complex is over 60ft (18.2m) high. The castle, which contains fine medieval armour and tapestries, is open on Sundays and BH from Easter to October and daily (not Saturdays) in high summer.

The gate is tall as it guards the edge of the deer park here at Eastnor. Use the tall kissing-gate and take the middle one of the three tracks beyond, climbing gradually to reach the Obelisk, an eye-catching feature at the heart of the park. This was built in 1812, principally as a memorial to the son of the first Earl Somers who was killed in the Peninsular War.

A Return from the Obelisk to the high gate and take the wooded track opposite, signed for Gullet car park. This is soon reached; the flooded quarry and immense, blasted rock faces cut from some of

the oldest rocks in Britain, Precambrian gneiss over 600 million years old.

Put your back to the quarry and look to the low sign banning wheeled vehicles. To the right of this, a wide path starts up into the woods. This is initially steep but eases after a while as it rises through the trees. Ignore any paths off to the left or right and stay on the main path. This eventually reaches a T-junction at the edge of the woods; turn right along the grassy path that passes through ramparts to reach Hollybush Hill, one of the twin summits of

Deer in Eastnor Park

? *What does the shelter within the ramparts commemorate?*

Midsummer Hill. These ramparts are the ditches of an Iron Age hill fort; turn left to reach the summit. Virtually all the summits of the Malverns have such a feature; the best preserved is that on Herefordshire Beacon, a mile or so to the north.

The views are stupendous – west to the Black Mountains and Brecon Beacons, south to the Forest of Dean, east to the Cotswolds, north to the Clee Hills, with all points in between holding distant hills and vales, and a fine view up the spine of the Malverns towards Worcestershire Beacon.

B Head south, passing by the shelter to pick up a well-walked path down through the fort's corrugated ramparts. This enters ash and oak woods, steepening as it falls towards a pasture, at the foot of which is the car park. ●

Almeley

START Almeley
(grid ref: SO 336516)
DISTANCE 2½ miles (4km)
TIME 1½ hours
PARKING Almeley village
hall
ROUTE FEATURES Easy
walking on back lanes
and field paths; about 12
stiles and gates

*This secluded little village is mentioned in
the famous Domesday survey of 1086 as a
large holding owned by Roger de Laci, an
influential Norman knight. Much of these
days of yore survives, including the
remains of two castles, a manor and a fine
old church. This easy walk meanders through this
history, rising on pleasant field paths and lanes to
reveal lovely views of the undulating countryside
and the distant line of the imposing Black
Mountains.*

*Old fishponds, castle mound and manor
house, Almeley*

From the village hall take the
road across the village green, the
cricket pitch to your left, to a T-
junction. Look opposite for a stile
and walk left around two sides of
this field, ignoring the stile in the
first corner. Just in from the
second corner is a stile beside a
gate; take this and go ahead, fence
on your left. Pass by a stile beside a
finger-post, keeping ahead beside
the fence. Look back for
impressive views across to the
Black Mountains and Brecon
Beacons. As this fence turns left,

PUBLIC TRANSPORT None suitable
REFRESHMENTS Pub in Almeley
PUBLIC TOILETS None
ORDNANCE SURVEY MAPS Explorer 201 (Knighton & Presteigne)

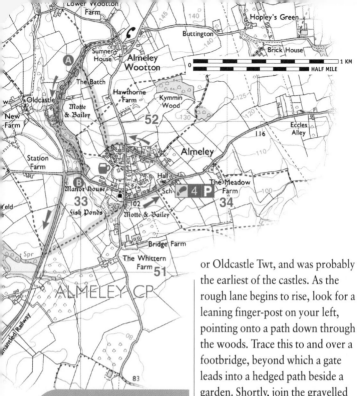

walk directly ahead across the field to a stile through a fence and carry straight on to reach a steep bank. Look to the foot of this for steps onto a footbridge across a brook.

Ⓐ Turn left along the rough lane. Pass by a cottage, behind which is the mound of one of Almeley's two castles. It is known locally as Batch,

or Oldcastle Twt, and was probably the earliest of the castles. As the rough lane begins to rise, look for a leaning finger-post on your left, pointing onto a path down through the woods. Trace this to and over a footbridge, beyond which a gate leads into a hedged path beside a garden. Shortly, join the gravelled driveway and walk through to a minor road.

Ⓑ Turn right along the lane. As you round the bend a ruined building takes the eye to the field above. This is all that remains of Almeley station which finally closed in 1940.

Pass between the old bridge abutments then turn left towards Eardisley. In about 600 yds (548m), just before woods, take

The railway was built largely along the line of an early tram road. **The Kington and Eardisley Tramway** was built between 1818 and 1820, connecting a foundry in Kington and quarries at Burlingjobb to another tramway at Eardisley, from here linking through to Brecon. The horse-drawn line survived for over 50 years before being taken over and replaced by the Great Western line in 1874. A 'plate', a section of old tram track, is preserved in the Tram Inn in nearby Eardisley.

the waymarked stile, left, into an orchard. Look half left to the far side for another stile into pasture and then walk ahead in line just right of the church, crossing a stile through a fence to reach a

footbridge and, beyond, reedy hollows. These are the remains of the fishponds that served the motte-and-bailey castle, the imposing remains of which tower above. The old house beyond is the medieval village manor.

Head for the lowest cottage ahead to find a stile into a lane. Turn left. Take time to visit the lovely old St Mary's Church, within which is a rare painted 'Tudor Rose' ceiling some 500 years old. Look, too, for an old AA village name sign on a barn. To return to the village hall, take the lane virtually opposite the lychgate, signed for Sarnesfield, Weobley and Leominster. ●

Almeley village

5 *Longtown*

START Longtown
(grid ref: SO 324287)
DISTANCE 3 miles (4.8km)
TIME 1½ hours
PARKING Longtown parish
hall
ROUTE FEATURES Field
paths; lanes

*With the sturdy remains of an old castle,
fine views and a remarkable old church,
this walk in the upper Monnow valley is an
easy and comprehensive introduction to
the Black Mountains and the secluded
communities that characterise the area. The
hills and woods are an artist's palette of
colours throughout the year, whilst buzzards,
kestrels and sparrowhawks add interest with
their aerial displays.*

Turn left from the car park
and walk up the road to reach the
village green. Up a drive to the left
are the remains of Longtown
Castle.

Return to the road and turn
downhill to reach, in 200 yds
(183m), a triangular junction and a
lane branching right. Follow this to
a low bridge across the Olchon
Brook. Just before this, look up left
for a waymarked stile and trace the
hedge on the right to a footbridge

Village church and pub, Clodock

PUBLIC TRANSPORT None suitable
REFRESHMENTS Pub and shop in Longtown, pub at Clodock
PUBLIC TOILETS None
ORDNANCE SURVEY MAPS Explorer OL13 (Brecon Beacons National Park –
Eastern Area)

across the brook. Cross this and head half left to a waymarked stile below an oak tree halfway along the distant hedge line. Take this and walk ahead, aiming for the break of slope in the ridge of Hatterrall Hill.

Cross a stiled footbridge near the corner and cut half right to a waymarked field gate and then a further one in line with a barn. From this stile, head half left to a walker's gate in the hedgerow, then look half right for a gate and

Whilst many castles were built during the Norman period, relatively few were developed to the stage of having stone buildings. **Longtown** is one such; built for the influential **de Lacy family** in the 12th century it has the oldest circular keep still standing in this area. It was designed as the heart of a 'planted' borough 'Ewyas Lacy', aimed at profiting from agricultural and trade taxes. Such dreams, however, never came to fruition and the castle gradually fell into disrepair. Legend has it that a tunnel runs beneath the Black Mountains from the castle to Llanthony Priory!

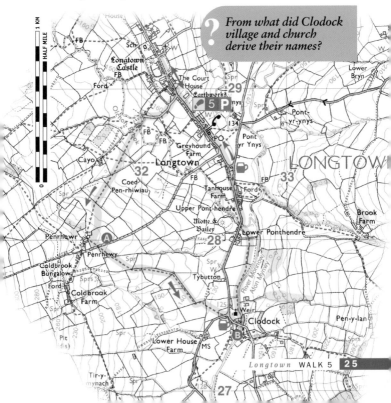

? From what did Clodock village and church derive their names?

Clodock Church below Mynydd Merddin

finger-post. Drop down the drive to a lane.

A Cross to a waymarked gate into pasture. Look half right, downslope, for a stile roughly in line with the church tower, climb this and head half left for a stile in the far bottom corner, guarded by a stone slab. Turn left beyond this, pass through a gate and drop to two metal gates in a corner. Take neither; instead turn right to a stile onto a sloping footbridge. Keep to the left of the field to reach another footbridge, cross this and turn left to a stile into a dingle. Go straight through and then look half right for a stile onto a road.

B Turn left to reach Clodock Church. This amazing old building has some medieval wall paintings, lovely old pews and a spectacular pulpit, behind which is a memorial stone dating from about AD830.

Next to the church is the completely unspoilt Cornewall Arms, well worth a visit. At the north east corner of the churchyard find a slab-stile made from an old gravestone and join the fenced path beyond, with the River Monnow on your right. Several more waymarked stiles and gates bring you to a large stone slab-stile. Take this and bend left alongside the old orchard to reach the road. Turn right and then keep left at the junction to return to the start. ●

Above Clodock

Shobdon

START Shobdon Church
(grid ref: SO 401629)
DISTANCE 3 miles (4.8km)
TIME 2 hours
PARKING Shobdon
Church. From the B4362
just east of the village
follow the brown 'Tourist'
signs for Shobdon Arch
and Church Visitor
Centre
ROUTE FEATURES Easy
walking on back lanes;
field paths; about 14
stiles. *Beware flying golf
balls on the golf course*

*Set amidst a pastoral landscape of soft
fruit orchards and cornfields below the
wooded ridge of Shobdon Hill, the village
has an airfield popular with skydivers, so
keep half an eye on the skies on this walk.
The true treasure of Shobdon is lost
amidst a huge landscaped parkland above
the village; an eccentric and unforgettable
church mixing rococo and Gothic-revival
styles. The walk passes this and also
allows excellent views of the tumbled hills
and commons of the borderland with Radnorshire.*

Walk up the avenue of trees
(cricket pitch on your right) – your
target is the arched structure at the
top. This is all that remains of the
original Norman church;
Romanesque arches and doorways
from the chancel of the 800-year-
old building, placed here as a folly
in the 1750s. The intricate stone
carvings are now weathering away.
Take time to drink in the enormous
views across to the Black Mountains
and the peaks of the Brecon
Beacons. Facing these arches, turn
left for 50 paces before bending

The Norman arches in Shobdon Park

right with the wide path into the
copse. Trace this through the trees
to reach a tarred lane.

PUBLIC TRANSPORT Infrequent buses to Shobdon from Leominster and Kington
REFRESHMENTS Pub and shops in Shobdon; café at visitor centre
PUBLIC TOILETS At visitor centre
ORDNANCE SURVEY MAPS Explorers 201 (Knighton & Presteigne) and 203 (Ludlow)

The traditional external appearance of **St John's Church** disguises an interior that stuns every visitor. A confection of icing sugar decoration that is highest rococo Gothic assaults the eye, a heady mix of pastel blue and white quite unlike any other village church. It was built for **Lord Bateman** in the 1750s to replace the original church, held by many to be amongst the best early Norman buildings in the country. Of this, just the tower and font remain.

A Turn left along this peaceful lane and follow it for nearly one mile (1.6km). At a sharp left bend, a driveway leads right to Belgate Farm. Our route, however, is through the gateway on the inside of the corner, waymarked as a foot-path and circular walk. It's worth pausing here to enjoy the views to the heights of Radnor Forest and the distinctive hill of Whimble.

B Take the gate and cross to a stile in line with powerlines, then continue half left to a wide stile through a high hedge. Accompany the fence above Downwood Farm to a stile, right. Take this, go ahead to climb another and turn left. Turn right immediately before the next stile to reach a field corner near a pond. Go left over a stile and follow the field edge, soon cutting half right to reach a wooded corner and a waymarked stile. Climb it and walk beside the trees (right); the path soon bends left alongside a

The old donkey cider press on Shobdon Green

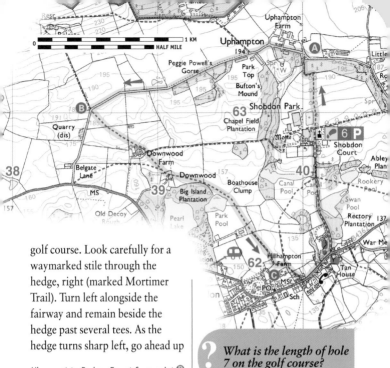

golf course. Look carefully for a waymarked stile through the hedge, right (marked Mortimer Trail). Turn left alongside the fairway and remain beside the hedge past several tees. As the hedge turns sharp left, go ahead up

View west to Radnor Forest from point Ⓑ

? *What is the length of hole 7 on the golf course?*

along the strip of immature trees, drifting to the right of the fairway alongside a high hedge.

Ⓒ Take the stile in the corner and turn left to climb another two. Once over, turn right to find an enclosed path beside a house, leading to the village street. Turn left and walk to the Bateman Arms. Carefully cross to the left here and take the driveway between the gateposts, which will return you to the church and car park. ●

7 *Ruckhall*

START Clehonger (grid ref: SO 452377)
DISTANCE 3 miles (4.8km)
TIME 1½ hours
PARKING Clehonger village hall, (off Birch Hill Road)
ROUTE FEATURES Field paths; back lanes

A wooded sandstone bluff just west of Hereford offers good views up the valley of the River Wye, best appreciated from the tables outside the old inn here. This easy, undulating walk also offers glimpses of an Iron Age hill fort, passes by old mills and rises to a low ridge between Ruckhall and Clehonger, revealing a grand panorama to the north and west beyond the space age dishes of a satellite ground station.

Walk past the hall to the road. Turn left and cross to a stile beyond a phone box. Take the field path ahead to a derelict stile in the corner above woods (left). Keep to the left of the next field; near the end take the waymarked gap in the hedge and drop to a brick structure beside the brook. Cross the brook and keep left at a waymarked post, on a path into marshy pasture.

A At the end cross the footbridge and turn right above the brook. Climb a stile into a large field below New Barns Farm. As the stream bends away, cut the corner

If you're lucky you may see a **red kite** circling above the Wye Valley here. These magnificent birds are scavengers, feeding on carrion. They were persecuted to near extinction in the 1960s, with just a few pairs surviving in Mid Wales. Conservation measures have seen the population rise, and these birds are now spreading into the Marches from their heartland on the upper Wye. They're easily recognised by their reddish-brown feathers and distinctive forked tail.

PUBLIC TRANSPORT Buses to Clehonger from Hereford
REFRESHMENTS Pub in Clehonger; the Ancient Camp Inn at Ruckhall
PUBLIC TOILETS None
ORDNANCE SURVEY MAPS Explorer 189 (Hereford & Ross-on-Wye)

to a stile and field gate. Turn right along the lane.

At the junction turn left for Ruckhall. Climb this lane, which levels beside orchards. The distinct bank beyond the trees is the rampart of an Iron Age hill fort.

Bend left with the road, then turn right at the phone box along a lane signed for the Ancient Camp Inn. Walk to the entrance to the inn car park.

The view towards Ruckhall

B Turn left along the enclosed path to a waymarked post; here turn right on a ledged path outside the pub grounds. To your left are splendid views up the Wye, which sweeps below this wooded river cliff.

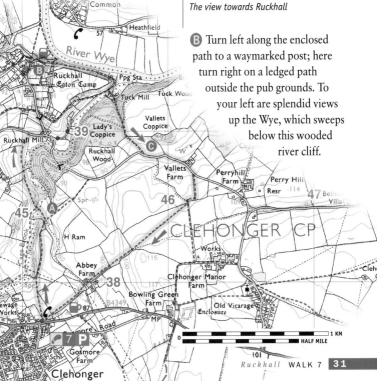

The River Wye from the Ancient Camp Inn, Ruckhall

Cross the steps down from the pub and carry on ahead into the woods. Climb a flight of steps leading up, then shortly a flight down, continuing below mature pines and oaks.

> **?** *How many steps are there in these two flights?*

Drop to the riverbank and walk downstream. Pass right of the old pumping station and then turn right along a track to a gate. Turn left over the bridge to pass Tuck Mill cottage and house. Now go through the gate just beyond Mill House and up the woodland path to a gate into pasture. Skirt the woods to another gate and walk the field road to a lane.

C Turn left and pass Vallets Farm. In 100 yds (91m) take the stile, right, into a field and climb to a corner stile by a dead tree. Turn right to use a third stile, left. Head half right across the vast field, at the far corner another stile leads into a sloping field. Views from this corner are excellent, across to the Black Mountains and, closer to hand, the radio telescopes at Madley Earth Station.

Walk down to the corner and slip just right of the hedged track to drop to a wooden barn. Pass right of this, then look left for a way-marked gate (the higher of two) into an orchard. Keep to the left to a kissing-gate; then walk to the corner beyond the houses, opposite which is the village hall. ●

Weobley

START Weobley
(grid ref: SO 402518)
DISTANCE 3¼ miles
(5.2km)
TIME 1½ hours
PARKING Village car park
off Bell Square, at the
north west corner of the
town
ROUTE FEATURES Lanes;
farm roads; field paths

Weobley is the archetypical chocolate box village, a heady mix of half-timbered cottages, inns, farms and manors huddled between an old castle mound and the high spired medieval village church. The walk leaves exploring this until the end, first charting an easy course past a remarkable Elizabethan farmhouse and offering grand views across much of the west of the county.

From the car park turn left along Bell Square. Turn first left along Church Street and walk to the church. Dedicated to St Peter and St Paul, it has the second highest spire in Herefordshire.

The most striking monument in the church is the marble memorial to Colonel John Birch. It shows him wearing the **Roundhead armour of the Civil War** when, as a commander in Cromwell's army, he captured Hereford. He also was a signatory to the death warrant of King Charles I. He is mentioned in *Samuel Pepys' Diary* as one who planned the rebuilding of London after the Great Fire. He retired to Weobley and became the town's MP.

Rejoin Church Street and walk to the bend where a stile, left, leads into pasture. Stick to the left of this field, cross the slab bridge and walk on along the field edge to an enclosed path leading through to Meadow Street. Turn left; in 100 yds (91m) look for a waymarked stile and field gate on the right. Walk along this sunken track, take the stile at the end and head for the opposite top corner to another stile and, in a further 50 paces, use a third stile on your right beside a water trough.

Skirt the fence to a farther stile into a large field. Go straight ahead to a

PUBLIC TRANSPORT Buses to Weobley from Hereford and Leominster
REFRESHMENTS Pubs, shops and cafés in Weobley
PUBLIC TOILETS Near Weobley library
ORDNANCE SURVEY MAPS Explorers 201 (Knighton & Presteigne) and 202
(Leominster & Bromyard)

stile beyond the offset corner. Keeping ahead, several more stiles bring you to a paddock in front of the magnificent farmhouse, The Ley.

A Walk past the house and into the farmyard where waymark arrows show the way to a concreted farm road. As this fails, look on the right for a stile, climb it and turn left, soon to walk alongside a hedge. Cross the plank bridge in the field corner and head slightly right to an offset field corner, here put the hedge on your left and walk through to the woodland edge.

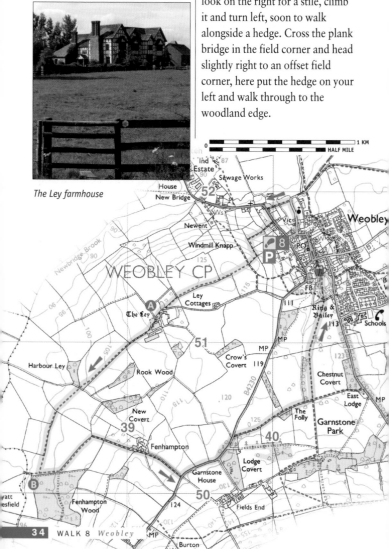

The Ley farmhouse

High Street and the Unicorn Inn, Weobley

B Turn left along the track and remain on this as it curves away from the trees in about 200 yds (183m). On gaining a wider, hedged farm lane turn right and walk to and through the farmyard at Fenhampton Farm to a road. Turn left along this; there's no verge, so exercise caution, although the sight lines are good. A wide verge develops beside a covert, at the far end of which take the waymarked track to the right.

Stay on this track for about ½ mile (800m). You'll pass by a 'Conservation Walks' disc and then a 'Permissive Path' disc on your left; walk a farther 100 yds (91m) to

turn left along a wide dirt track down the middle of a field. The spire of Weobley Church is ahead. Take a kissing-gate and go slightly right towards the left of a wooden building. Here a gate leads into the substantial remains of Weobley's old castle. At the far end a path leads to the top of Broad Street. The green at the heart of the old village is the site of cottages destroyed by fire in 1943. At the foot of the street turn left at the Red Lion to return to the car park. ●

> **?** *Which powerful family first built Weobley Castle?*

9 *The Biblins*

This walk visits the most spectacular section of the Wye Gorge. Two crossings of the river, by bridge and by boat, add a flavour of adventure. There's a chance, too, for a trip on the river and tantalising glimpses of how our Neolithic forefathers lived. There are sheer, unprotected drops near to the start of this walk. Take extreme care in damp weather and ensure that children and pets are kept under close supervision. *Before setting out, ring the Saracen's Head (01600 890435) to check that the ferry is working – it operates, on demand, on most days of the year.*

START The Doward (grid ref: SO 547156)
DISTANCE 3½ miles (5.6km)
TIME 2 hours
PARKING Forest Enterprise car park, Great Doward. From Ross take the A40 south to the exit past the Symonds Yat West turn, signed for Stoney Hill, Crocker's Ash and Doward. Turn right, uphill to Crocker's Ash and turn left at a sign for 'Biblins and Doward Park Campsite'. At the campsite, drive down the forestry road for 100m and park on the right
ROUTE FEATURES Woodland paths and tracks; riverside paths; back lanes. Some modest climbs and descents

Walk back to the tarred lane and fork left. In 109 yds (100m) turn back left along a wide path, shortly passing an interpretive board. Continue gently downhill, soon reaching the first of several caves hereabouts; the next one a little farther down the track is the more extensive King Arthur's Cave. Return to the main path and follow it away from the outcrops, keeping immediately left of the low waymark post. The path bends gradually left; go straight over a crossing path and through the beech and oak woods, an occasional

PUBLIC TRANSPORT None
REFRESHMENTS Pubs and teas at Symonds Yat East
PUBLIC TOILETS Symonds Yat East
ORDNANCE SURVEY MAPS Explorer OL14 (Wye Valley and Forest of Dean)

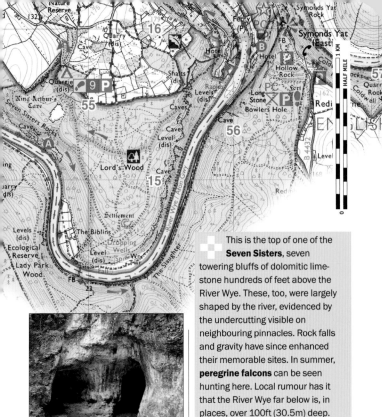

This is the top of one of the **Seven Sisters**, seven towering bluffs of dolomitic limestone hundreds of feet above the River Wye. These, too, were largely shaped by the river, evidenced by the undercutting visible on neighbouring pinnacles. Rock falls and gravity have since enhanced their memorable sites. In summer, **peregrine falcons** can be seen hunting here. Local rumour has it that the River Wye far below is, in places, over 100ft (30.5m) deep.

a most spectacular viewpoint. *Take great care here.*

Ⓐ Return to the main path and turn right, walking through to a junction of paths at a sloping clearing. Your route is straight

King Arthur's Cave

yellow arrow painted on a trunk confirming the way.

At the next fork marked by a post, keep left and scramble up a small outcrop onto a narrower path. Pass by a warning sign. In a farther 150 yds (137m) fork right at a waymark post and carefully walk through to

> **?** How many people can use the bridge at any one time?

ahead, up an exposure of rock onto a firm path through the woods. There are occasional views through the trees into the gorge. At the well graded forestry road turn right. At a fork keep right, dropping to the field centre at The Biblins. Keep left of this to gain the riverbank and then walk across the seemingly precarious wire swing bridge. This was built in the 1930s as an aid to forestry management.

At the far side, turn left and walk the forestry road/old railway track through to Symonds Yat East. Pleasure cruiser trips operate from here, usually between Easter and autumn.

Ⓑ Catch the rope ferry (small fee) from outside the Saracen's Head Inn and climb the steps at the far side. Turn left along the rough lane and follow it down, then around a hairpin bend and more steeply uphill. Remain on this for 500 yds (457m) to reach a cottage on your left called Forest End. Turn sharp left here along a waymarked green track, tracing this into the woods.

Passing by old quarry workings, the path rises to a fork a short way beyond a Woodland Trust sign. Fork right and ignore any paths off to the left or right. You'll eventually reach the end of a graded forestry road; walk along this. Keep right at the fork and walk up to meet a wider forestry road, turning right to return to the car park.　●

The footbridge over the Wye at The Biblins

The Golden Valley

START Peterchurch (grid ref: SO 345386)

DISTANCE 4 miles (6.4km)

TIME 2 hours

PARKING Peterchurch picnic area; down the lane beside the Boughton Arms pub

ROUTE FEATURES Back lanes; field paths

10

*The Golden Valley is one of the most tranquil places in the county, a wide vale laced by lanes and tracks, dotted with hamlets and villages and bounded by the first upwellings of the Black Mountains and low, wooded ridges and commons.
This walk starts from the 'capital' of the valley, rising easily to the site of one of the many defensive sites in the area and offering tremendous views across rolling acres of sheep pasture and golden cornfields to distant hills and mountains.*

Despite its name, the Golden Valley takes its name from the Welsh 'dwr' – water, referring to the River Dore that has carved this delightfully unspoilt vale east of the Black Mountains, rather than from the French for golden, 'd'or'.

🖉 From the car park turn right, pass by the churchyard gate and cross the bridge. At the far end go left along the tarred footpath, which soon swings right and traces a course past a farm to a minor road. Turn right along this and walk through to the crossroads. Turn left along Long Lane, soon starting a gradual climb past a

The old Norman chapel at Urishay

PUBLIC TRANSPORT Peterchurch is on the Hereford to Hay bus route

REFRESHMENTS Pubs and shops in Peterchurch

PUBLIC TOILETS None

ORDNANCE SURVEY MAPS Explorer OL13 (Brecon Beacons National Park – Eastern area)

Urishay Castle was one of countless fortified sites built to defend against the marauding Welsh in Norman times. It decayed in more peaceful times, and the site was usurped by a grand Jacobean house, the remains of which stand gaunt and jackdaw-haunted today on the old motte. The tiny chapel is contemporary with the Norman castle; until fairly recently it was used as a barn. All are on private land.

string of cottages and houses. You'll pass by Nurse's Cottage on your left; about 150 yds (137m) after this, take the finger-posted stile on the left and walk across the pasture to a couple of stiles either side of a track here at Hostley's Farm.

A Go ahead between the breeze block buildings. Immediately beyond these, look for the

waymarked ladder-stile on the left, beyond which take two further stiles (the second at a displaced plank bridge over a ditch). Put the wire fence and a ditch on your left and walk up the pasture, aiming for the line of trees on the low ridge ahead. Gaining this ridge, cross the stile and take time to admire the fine views across to Hatterrall Ridge, the edge of the Black Mountains.

Look slightly right downslope for a wide field gate and drop to this, go through it and head half right to use a stile in the hedge. Walk to the

Oatley Farm and the Golden Valley

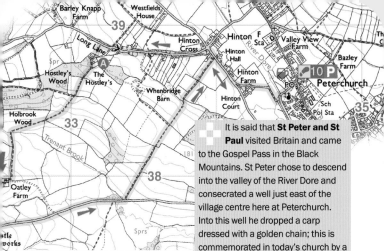

It is said that **St Peter and St Paul** visited Britain and came to the Gospel Pass in the Black Mountains. St Peter chose to descend into the valley of the River Dore and consecrated a well just east of the village centre here at Peterchurch. Into this well he dropped a carp dressed with a golden chain; this is commemorated in today's church by a plaque high on one wall (directly opposite the door you enter by). The church itself is notable for some exquisite Norman architecture – and for its remarkable fibreglass spire.

far left corner and a footbridge across Trenant Brook. Climb the left side of the next field to another footbridge, cross and turn right to rise to Oatley Farm. Walk through the farmyard to join the rough access road.

B At the end, pause to admire the wonderful views east down the Golden Valley (as far as the Malverns) before turning left, then left again at the nearby junction. Along this lane you'll pass the gated entrance to Urishay Castle Farm (private, no access).

Remain on the lane for one mile (1.6km). Just as it starts to rise beyond a bridge, take the waymarked path, left, through the left set of two gates and walk right, up the field edge. Take a gate and continue up to a stile on the ridge, then go ahead to a stile in the fence. Walk slightly left down the pasture, just left of the pylons, to a stile beneath trees in an offset corner. Take this and turn right, picking a gap through the thorn hedge to walk to and through the old orchard to the house driveway. From this turn right along the lane, then fork left at the 'No Through Road' to return to the church. ●

? *In which year was this spire erected, and how much did it cost?*

11 *Merbach Hill*

A long, undulating ridge separates the Golden Valley from the Wye Valley here in the far west of Herefordshire. This walk takes full advantage of this morphology, starting from a remarkable prehistoric site and culminating in what is undoubtedly the best viewpoint on the entire length of the Wye Valley Walk, the snout of Merbach Hill. The route then follows a stretch of the waymarked recreational trail before threading back on field paths to the start.

START Arthur's Stone (grid ref: SO 318432)

DISTANCE 4 miles (6.4km)

TIME 2 hours

PARKING Arthur's Stone which is signposted by brown 'Tourist' road signs from both Dorstone and Bredwardine *(warning – very narrow lanes)*

ROUTE FEATURES Quiet lanes; sheep pasture; field paths; farm tracks

🖉 We start at a most poignant site above Dorstone, where the remains of an ancient burial chamber are set on a ridgetop. Who knows whether our distant ancestors also valued the vistas from such a location and chose to bury their dead here.

Walk along the lane, putting the burial chamber to your left. The long, straight, undulating road already offers excellent views, just a hint of what is to come. Continue

Arthur's Stone is the remains of a communal burial chamber dating back to the Neolithic (New Stone Age) era over 5000 years ago. Old records show that an oval mound over 18 metres long once covered the fractured stones seen today. The huge capstone weighs 25 tons and is supported on wall stones, a structure also known as a cromlech. The name Arthur's Stone has nothing to do with the Dark Ages hero; it is more likely to be a corruption of 'Thor's Stone', suggesting some later, pagan use of this site by Scandinavian settlers.

PUBLIC TRANSPORT None

REFRESHMENTS None en route; pubs in Dorstone and Bredwardine both 1½ miles (2.4km) from the start

PUBLIC TOILETS None

ORDNANCE SURVEY MAPS Explorers 201 (Knighton & Presteigne) and OL13 (Brecon Beacons National Park – Eastern area)

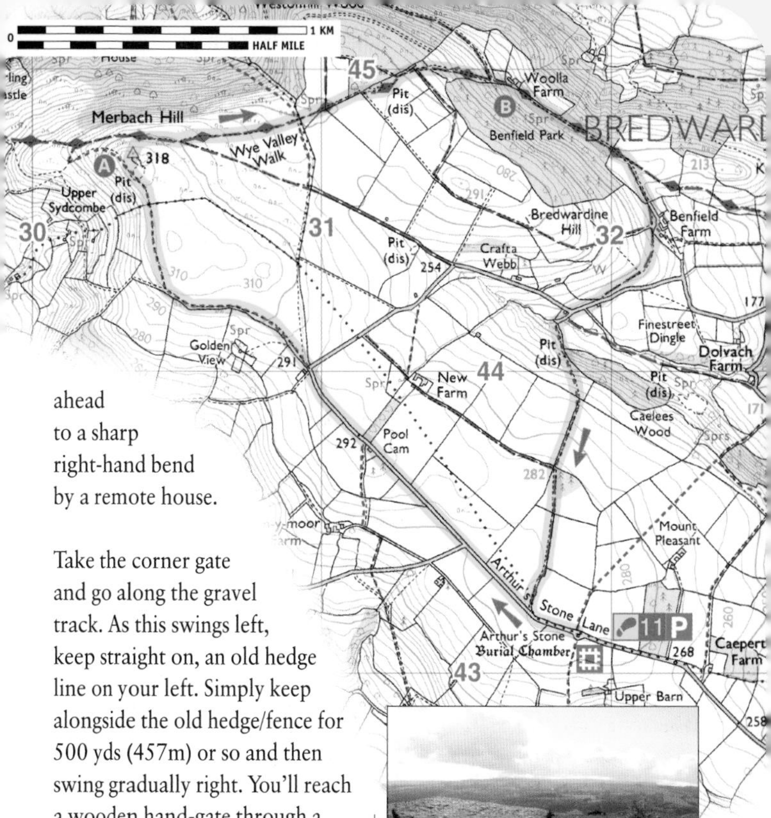

ahead
to a sharp
right-hand bend
by a remote house.

Take the corner gate
and go along the gravel
track. As this swings left,
keep straight on, an old hedge
line on your left. Simply keep
alongside the old hedge/fence for
500 yds (457m) or so and then
swing gradually right. You'll reach
a wooden hand-gate through a
fence, beyond which pick a route
across this rough land to reach the
triangulation pillar at the top of
Merbach Hill.

Ⓐ The views are spectacular.
Below, the Wye meanders around
some of its great loops. To the
north are Hergest Ridge and
Radnor Forest; south and west are
the stunning ridges and scarps of
the Black Mountains, with the
Brecon Beacons beyond these.

*Arthur's Stone cromlech and distant
Black Mountains*

Farther south east are the Vale of
Usk and Monmouthshire, the
Forest of Dean Plateau and the line
of the Cotswolds. Far to the east
are the Malvern Hills, whilst
farther north are the Clee Hills and

the distant peaks of the Long Mynd.

What is the reference number of the triangulation pillar on Merbach Hill?

Put your back to the pillar face with the plaque at its base, facing east-north-east towards the distant Malverns. Take the path bending half left into an area of thorns and bracken. This falls down to a way-mark post with a Wye Valley Walk disc attached. Turn right along this path and walk through the scrubby birch woods to reach a gate just beyond a waymarked cross-path.

Go through the gate and ahead through further gates into a fenced track beside a spinney (left). At the end continue ahead to pass right of a barn, drop to the field track and cross over, joining a steep field road down towards Woolla Farm.

B Immediately above the farm, take the waymarked hand-gate on the right; a narrow path winds through the woodland edge above the farm to gain the driveway beyond. Remain on this over a cattle grid and through to Benfield Farm.

Keep right on a tarred road past the barn. Look to your right for two gates and take the left one into a sunken track. This issues into a sloping field; bend gradually right around the shoulder to a waymarked gate near a cottage. Turn right along the lane.

At the bend by the next cottage slip left along the waymarked track and walk to a stile at the end. Turn left and join a path just above the edge of the woods. Before reaching a line of old thorn trees striking across the field, climb right, up to a stile through a hedge. Aim now for the pines on the low ridge top, using a gate in the corner to join a bridlepath. Head half left past the pines to another gate; from here trace the left field edge to gain a lane. Turn left to return to Arthur's Stone. ●

The Black Mountains from Merbach Hill

Edvin and Edwyn

START Edvin Loach
(grid ref: SO 663585)
DISTANCE 4¼ miles
(6.8km)
TIME 2 hours
PARKING Edvin Loach
church car park (signed
along lanes off the
B4203 north east of
Bromyard)
ROUTE FEATURES Field
paths; back lanes

Three remote churches secreted amongst the rolling countryside to the north of Bromyard Downs are the targets of this walk. Ranging from Saxon to Victorian in age, each has a story to tell, a heady mix of heroism, piety and larceny. The route offers far-reaching views across this corner of Herefordshire, rich farmland at the headwaters of the River Frome, an unsung waterway that flows all the way from this northern corner of the county to the River Wye near Hereford.

Edvin Loach has two churches; the small Victorian replacement and the ancient original. This latter was built shortly after the Norman Conquest in a style that recalled the church architecture of the Saxons and is thus often known as the Saxon Church. Of particular note is the herringbone pattern of many of the earliest walls still standing. The replacement St Mary's Church was built by a local businessman, William Barneby.

St Mary's Church hit the headlines thanks to the recovery of a small bell. The Victorian church made use of medieval bells from the older church; one of them dates from the 1340s and is one of the oldest in Britain. At New Year 1998, two of the three bells were stolen and all seemed lost. In 2003, however, an eagle-eyed bellringer at a church in Trowbridge noticed one of the **missing bells** on display in an estate agent's window in that Wiltshire town. It was duly returned to Edvin Loach and is displayed within. Its sister bell is still missing.

Walk back along the rough approach road. Off to your right, the Malverns draw the eye south beyond the heights of the nearby

PUBLIC TRANSPORT None
REFRESHMENTS All services in Bromyard 3½ miles (5.6km)
PUBLIC TOILETS None
ORDNANCE SURVEY MAPS Explorer 202 (Leominster & Bromyard)

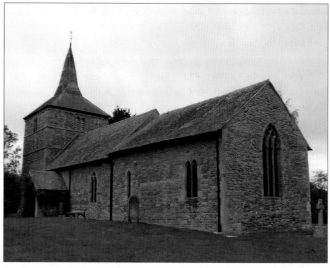

St Michael's Church, Edwyn Ralph

Bromyard Downs; to the north is Titterstone Clee Hill, capped by a radar dome. Turn right down the lane to reach Steeples Farm. Turn right up the lane opposite the postbox. Bend right with it, ignore the lane to the left instead taking the waymarked gateway on the left into a field.

Stick to the left of the field, passing right of an isolated cottage. Immediately past this, take the stile on the left and turn down the pasture to a kissing-gate into the thicket. A path drops down to a footbridge; head to a double stile near the house and walk up the tarred driveway.

Ⓐ At the T-junction turn right, following this quiet lane through to Brickhouse Farm. Take the bend and look right for a finger-post beside a small barn. Walk through the paddock and alongside the farm pond, remaining beside the brook to reach a waymarked gateway in the corner. Go through and turn left to climb a stile; then walk ahead towards the distant, squat spire of Edwyn Ralph Church. Take another stile and then head towards the right-hand

Which rector of the old church at Edvin Loach held tenure here for the longest period?

end of the rail fencing for another stile, then a gateway into a lane. Turn left to the church.

St Michael's Church dates from the late 12th century. Inside is one of the finest collections of effigy tombs in the county, including knights and a rare 'Pardon Monument' – offering a prayer to this was said to grant the supplicant up to 60 days' pardon of sins. (Use the right-hand light switch by the door). In the trees to the west of the churchyard is a motte-and-bailey castle, all that remains of a village that succumbed to the Black Death plague in AD1349.

B Return to the lane and turn right. Turn the corner at Townsend Farm and walk on to reach two finger-posts on your right. Use the gate at the second of these and bisect the field to a footbridge beneath trees. Keep ahead to a bridlegate through the distant hedge; once through this turn right. Take the gate at the corner and trace the field boundary, right, to another gate. Go through and turn left to reach a path junction at a brick bridge. Do not cross this, but turn left along the waymarked path, following the wide track beside the brook (right).

C At the gateway turn right, cross the bridge and take the gate, climbing to pass left of the ruined cottage. Join the gated field road beyond and follow this through to the minor road near New House Farm. Turn left to walk back to the signposted church access road. ●

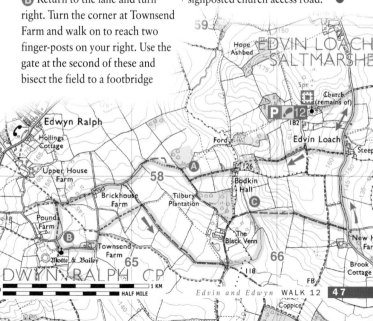

Edvin and Edwyn WALK 12 **47**

13 *Leintwardine*

START Leintwardine (grid ref: SO 404738)
DISTANCE 4¼ miles (6.8km)
TIME 2½ hours
PARKING Leintwardine village green, opposite The Lion Hotel
ROUTE FEATURES Village lanes; field paths; farm tracks and roads

The Rivers Teme and Clun confluence immediately west of Leintwardine; these waters are still occasionally used by coracles. This is an area of lush waterside meadows, wooded knolls and ridges that bristle with the sites of former motte-and-bailey castles, together with the stirring remains of a stone castle at nearby Wigmore. This walk traces field roads and paths from the heart of the village to modest heights offering splendid views across these middle Marches in the far north of Herefordshire.

Put your back to the village green and walk right, away from The Lion along Rosemary Lane. You'll soon pass by the tiny, remarkable Sun Inn. This is a real anachronism; just a couple of sparsely furnished little parlours and a scullery servery (there's no bar) where a barrel of beer and maybe cider stand. There are very, very few such beerhouses left; miss it at your peril.

Continue past the pub and along Rosemary Lane to the T-junction. Look to the left of the cottage opposite for a waymarked stile,

The Teme Bridge, Leintwardine

PUBLIC TRANSPORT Buses on the Ludlow to Knighton service call here
REFRESHMENTS Pubs and shop in Leintwardine
PUBLIC TOILETS None
ORDNANCE SURVEY MAPS Explorer 203 (Ludlow)

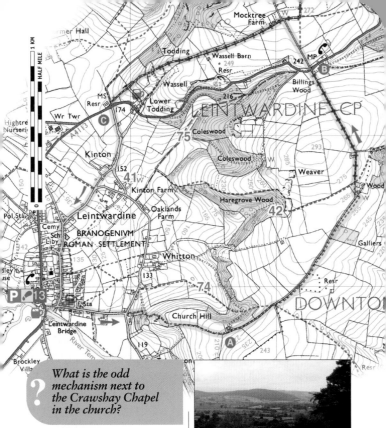

? What is the odd mechanism next to the Crawshay Chapel in the church?

take this and start a long, initially steep, but then gentle climb up Church Hill. You'll rise to an obvious field road that runs initially right before sweeping left up past an enormous old ash tree and beside old diggings.

Already, enough height has been gained to allow good views back across the village to the conifer clad hills of Clun Forest and

Distant Clun Forest

associated woodlands. To the south, the Teme meanders lazily past Brandon Hill (with a Roman camp) and near to the site of Wigmore Abbey, home abbey to the powerful Mortimer family, one of whom was crowned as King Edward IV.

Take a waymarked stile in the top corner of the field and walk ahead beside the line of old thorns. In 100 yds (91m) slip right into a wide grassy track, tracing this gradually uphill to reach a barn.

A From here, remain on the by now compacted farm road, continuing to gradually gain height. This track gently slips around to the right shoulder of the hillside, losing the views west but gaining a panorama to the east across the incised valley of the Teme at Downton to the steep, wooded hills of the Mortimer Forest, to Ludlow's commanding St Laurence's Church and castle and to the Clee Hills. At a fork keep ahead, climbing to the secluded farm and cottages at Woodhead.

Some way beyond here is another junction of tracks; here pick up the tarred lane ahead and rise with this to the crest, where through gaps in the hedgerow you can pick out the sharp hills of the Longmynd.

B The lane drops down to a main road. Carefully cross straight over and rise up the narrow lane to a T-junction where the tar gives way to gravel and earth. Turn left here and take the left-hand track, a rough hedged lane that passes by cottages. Beyond the final cottage this becomes an old green lane, sunken between high banks in a wooded strip. Passing by a farm, the lane becomes tarred; remain with it to reach the main road.

C Cross directly into a lane and walk with this through pleasant woodland. At a fork bear right along a dirt lane, falling with this past a delightful old thatched cottage to reach a minor road. Bear right to the top of Watling Street and turn left down this to return to the centre of Leintwardine. Along the way, divert right along Church Street to visit the fine medieval St Mary Magdalene Church, which stands partially across the line of the old Roman town wall. ●

Leintwardine occupies the site of the **Roman settlement** of **Branogenium**. Nothing remains of this, although the straight roads, including a branch of the famous Watling Street, recall these days and the village is set out on a grid pattern, perhaps also based on ancestral memory of these Latins. The medieval church contains superb choir stalls – carved oak misericords removed to here from Wigmore Abbey when it was suppressed during the reign of King Henry VIII.

How Caple and Yatton

The Wye Valley Walk follows a peaceful lane beside one of the river's gigantic, tight loops between Ross and Hereford; this walk joins the waymarked recreational footpath for a stretch before heading into the undulating, wooded countryside that typifies this corner of the county. Passing through landscaped parkland, the route rises along lanes to a remote hollow where a remarkable, tiny Norman church nestles in a farmyard. The last stages reveal fine views towards the Black Mountains.

14

START Hole-in-the-Wall (grid ref: SO 616294)
DISTANCE 4½ miles (7.2km)
TIME 2½ hours
PARKING Room for five cars at a lay-by near Lyndor, ½ mile (800m) north of Hole-in-the-Wall hamlet
ROUTE FEATURES Back lanes; field paths; farm tracks and field roads. One short stretch of busy road has good sight lines and verge for much of the way

🥾 Turn right along the lane, shortly passing by Lyndor. This is the route of the Wye Valley Walk, which stretches from the source of the river on Plynlimon, high in the Cambrian Mountains, to the mouth of the Wye below Chepstow. Beyond a cattle-grid, stay on the road to reach a sharp left-hand bend and, on the right, a finger-post pointing into parkland.

Rise through the meadow, aiming for the right side of the church which soon comes into view at the slope top. This is part of the How Caple Court estate. Take the gate beside the churchyard wall and turn left into the churchyard. The list of patrons goes back to 1279 here at St Andrew and St Mary's Church, although little remains of this early building, much restoration and development having taken place in Jacobean times. Much the same can be said of the court itself, a multi-gabled edifice with just hints of its medieval predecessor.

PUBLIC TRANSPORT None
REFRESHMENTS None en route; all services in Ross 3 miles (4.8km)
PUBLIC TOILETS None
ORDNANCE SURVEY MAPS Explorer 189 (Hereford & Ross-on-Wye)

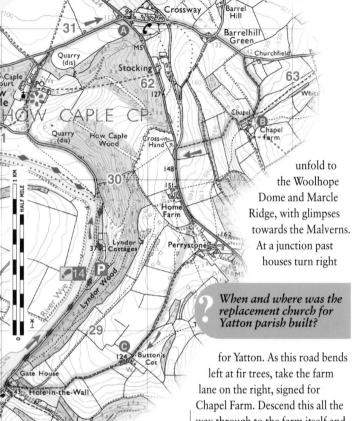

unfold to the Woolhope Dome and Marcle Ridge, with glimpses towards the Malverns. At a junction past houses turn right

? *When and where was the replacement church for Yatton parish built?*

for Yatton. As this road bends left at fir trees, take the farm lane on the right, signed for Chapel Farm. Descend this all the way through to the farm itself and the adjacent Yatton chapel.

B Walk back up the approach road for 100 yds (91m) to a waymarked gateway on the left. Enter this field and trace the left edge to a stile in the corner well beyond the chapel. Climb this and look upslope for a stile through the ridge-top fence; work your way up to this. Go straight across the next field to a waymarked path through

Walk up the driveway to a left-hand bend at a garage; here look right for an enclosed path which cuts near to a cottage to reach a lane. Turn right and follow it to the main road.

A Cross into the lane opposite, signed for Yatton and Much Marcle, and continue a gentle, easy climb. As the lane crests, nice views

This is one of several such farmyard churches in Herefordshire; there's another one at nearby Pixley. **Yatton chapel** dates from the 1100s, with a squat timbered belfry added in the 1500s. Long disused, it has a superb carved Norman doorway whilst inside some fine stone windows remain above the bare earth floor. Most medieval churches were like this; to add some comfort, protection and fragrancy, such floors would have been regularly strewn with straw or rushes. This is the origin of 'rush-bearing' ceremonies still held in some areas of Britain.

the woods. At the far side aim for the corrugated iron garage, in line with which a stile leads onto a road junction. Turn left along the main road. Cross to a narrow verge and take care whilst walking to and past Home Farm.

As the road bends left, take the waymarked track right, use the gate and walk ahead through the woods, ignoring a right fork. At the bend, enter the field ahead and walk just left of the little plantation to find a stile in the corner, left of the enormous, spreading oak. Turn right along the old drive here at the heart of the Perrystone estate. Ahead, the distant spire of Ross Church and the wooded hills beyond take the eye.

Ⓒ Pass by the cottage and fork right, putting the barn on your left. Angle left after the barn to join a fieldside track. Simply remain with this, hedge to your left, dropping gradually through the estate. Climb a stile beside a gate and follow the field road. At the end of the field look for a gate and stile into a sunken track; descend this to Hole-in-the-Wall. Turn right to return to the car park. ●

Chapel Farm and the old chapel, Yatton

● River ● woods ● views

15 *Bishop's Wood*

This walk is immediately upstream of the top of the famous Wye Gorge, where the Forest of Dean tumbles down from its plateau in a series of wooded hills and ridges to meet the Wye. The undulating Wye Valley Walk recreational footpath is followed for a while before the walk rises to lanes on Leys Hill, offering tantalising glimpses of the distant mountains and secluded dingles. The return is through the delightful Bishop's Wood, a route rich in woodland wildflowers in season.

START Kerne Bridge (grid ref: SO 582188)
DISTANCE 4½ miles (7.2km)
TIME 2 hours
PARKING Kerne Bridge Picnic Site and Canoe Launch (also signed as Bishop's Wood Village Hall)
ROUTE FEATURES Lanes; woodland paths and field roads. Muddy in places; modest climbs at start and near finish

From the back right of the car park a path cuts to the road and a bus shelter. Cross over into the lane and turn immediately left, up the drive for Old Forge Cottage. Go between cottages and up the steep steps into a sunken path. Bear right along the driveway to a cross drive; go straight across, up the waymarked Wye Valley Walk (WVW). Turn left along the tarred lane. In 200 yds (183m) turn left

? What is the logo of the Wye Valley Walk?

off this onto a grassy path (WVW) beside cupressus trees and then trace the surfaced lane downhill.

Ⓐ Just before the main road, turn right up a concrete track (WVW). As this turns right, go ahead on the path beneath trees. At the edge of the woods cross directly over the drive and along the WVW as a narrow path inside the woodland edge. Go straight over the tarred lane then pass left of Linden Lea House down grassy steps to a stile into meadows. Keep the fence left, cross another stile to rise steeply to

PUBLIC TRANSPORT Buses to Kerne Bridge from Ross-on-Wye and Monmouth
REFRESHMENTS The Inn on the Wye, Kerne Bridge
PUBLIC TOILETS None
ORDNANCE SURVEY MAPS Explorer OL14 (Wye Valley and Forest of Dean)

a stile into woods; cut through to a lane.

B Take the gravelled lane opposite (WVW), pass some houses and swing right in front of a double garage. At the complex junction of paths, leave the WVW and turn right up the concreted drive to pass beside a cottage. In 50 yds (46m) fork left up a wide track. At the top keep ahead along a rough lane to reach a minor road by an old chapel. Turn right and walk round a sharp bend to a T-junction.

C Turn right, then fork left along a level track (bridleway).

Remain on this past cottages to reach a rusty old gate. Here, fork right along the level path into the woods, then keep left at a fork along a wider track. Pass below a cottage, 'Roger's Well', and as the track loops left into a garden, fork right along a woodland path. In 100 yds (91m) take a path up to the left, passing a cottage to join a rough track leading to a tarred lane.

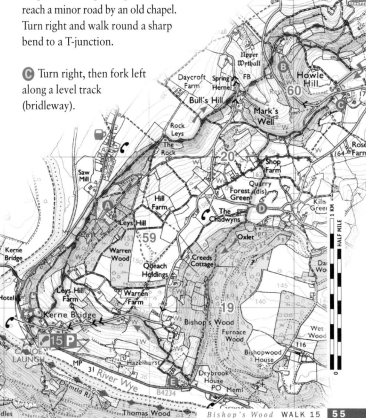

In Bishop's Wood

Go left along this for about 100 yds (91m) to a sharp right bend and a waymark post. Go ahead along the wide, hedged path to reach a left bend. Look on the right here for a stile, walk to the stables track and turn left to reach a road.

D Go down the rough lane opposite. Pass by the turn to

Chadwyn's Farm to reach a bend. Take the path, right, into the trees here; this soon widens to a delightful woodland path down through Bishop's Wood. Cross a stile and continue downhill, joining a brook on your left. The trees peel back and the path widens to a lane serving secluded cottages.

E At the foot of the lane, just before the main road, turn sharp right along a track outside an estate wall. Persevere through undergrowth and remain with this, eventually passing by a Romany caravan to emerge at a cross path. Turn right; in 50 yds (46m) fork left along the waymarked bridleway to reach a driveway at a cottage. Walk up this to reach a minor road. Turn left to return to the main road at Kerne Bridge and the car park. ●

Kerne Bridge itself, just upstream from the start of the walk, is a graceful sandstone structure that glows like an ember in certain lights. It was built in 1828 as a toll bridge, replacing a ferry. The Wye hereabouts was once criss-crossed by ferries. Just downstream was one operated by Royal Warrant, granted in 1388 by the soon-to-be Henry IV when he crossed to Courtfield (in the woods on the opposite bank to this walk) to visit his infant son, the future Henry V, who was raised, secure in this remote spot, by Lady Alice Salisbury.

The Arrow Valley

START Pembridge
(grid ref: SO 392583)
DISTANCE 4½ miles
(7.2km)
TIME 2½ hours
PARKING Pembridge
village car park, behind
the King's House pub
ROUTE FEATURES Village
roads; riverside and field
paths; back lanes

*Herefordshire is famed for its black and
white villages; this walk links two of the
best of these. The streets of Pembridge are
lined with higgledy-piggledy old cottages
and houses huddled between the old
church and ancient bridge across the River
Arrow. A pleasant walk through cornfields
and riverside pastures leads to Eardisland,
another jigsaw of impossibly scenic cottages
and an imposing riverside dovecote.*

Turn right from the car park
to reach the centre of Pembridge.
Turn left at the idyllic New Inn to
reach the remarkable medieval
market hall, supported on eight
wizened oak pillars. From here,
paths rise to St Mary's Church,
with its detached bell tower. Inside
the church are some fine alabaster
effigy tombs. The imposing
shingled bell tower is particularly
strong as it was used as a place of
refuge where villagers could shelter
when threatened by raids from the
Welsh.

Take the path directly away from
the porch to steps beside the shop
and walk down the road for
Shobdon, opposite. This falls
gently to the narrow bridge across
the Arrow. Turn right immediately
before this along a riverside track.
At the bend take the stile beside the
gate on the left, picking up a path
that angles a little right, leaving the
river to meander slightly to the
north.

Ⓐ At the far end of this long
pasture look mid-hedge for a

PUBLIC TRANSPORT Buses to Pembridge from Leominster, Kington and Hereford
REFRESHMENTS Pubs, cafés and shops in Pembridge and Eardisland
PUBLIC TOILETS Pembridge
ORDNANCE SURVEY MAPS Explorers 201 (Knighton & Presteigne) and 202
(Leominster & Bromyard)

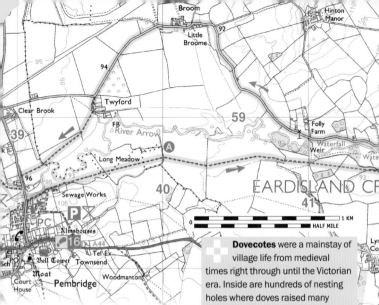

Dovecotes were a mainstay of village life from medieval times right through until the Victorian era. Inside are hundreds of nesting holes where doves raised many broods each year. The meat of young doves (squabs) was highly prized, whilst the eggs could also be sold. The guano (droppings) was used as a fertiliser, as an ingredient in the manufacture of saltpetre (a constituent of gunpowder) and in processing animal skins where it was useful in helping to remove hair!

footbridge across a ditch, to join an obvious path directly across the next field to another stile, then ahead left across a further field towards the tallest trees in the distance. A stile near gnarled oaks heralds a return to smaller meadows linked by a series of easily found stiles. A weir on your left is where the mill leat for Eardisland Mill takes water from the Arrow.

Another long pasture is soon joined. Head for the far end where

> *The unusual design of the bell tower at Pembridge Church is based on such towers commonly found in which north European country?*

it narrows into a tangle of trees and bushes. Look on the right for a double stile through a hedge, climb this and turn left, the tower of Eardisland Church coming into view. Another stile beneath an ash tree leads to a double stile and footbridge, beyond which walk past the stub end of a hedge to two further stiles leading into a lane at the heart of Eardisland. Turn left to reach the centre.

Again, take time to explore the village. St Mary's Church stands on the site of the original Saxon church. Next to this is a moated motte, the remains of the Norman castle, whilst next to the old river bridge is an imposing brick dovecote.

B The return route to Pembridge commences at this dovecote. Take the lane here, with the river to your right. This dog-legs left away from the grassy waterside banks to leave the village behind, soon crossing the River Arrow. Now simply follow this lane for the next 2 miles (3.2km). It's a quiet thoroughfare with only occasional farm traffic disturbing the tranquility. The tree-lined course of the Arrow snakes away to your left whilst ahead and right are views to the wooded hills and knolls that characterise this area of Herefordshire.

Cross a bridge over a brook and walk a long straight to reach a right-hand bend. Here go ahead beneath pine trees and along the driveway for Twyford. In 50 yds (46m) take the waymarked gate, right, through the ornate iron fencing, heading across the paddock for a gate in the far hedgerow. In the next large field aim for the far left corner, just in field from which is a narrow footbridge below a tree. Once over this walk slightly left of the line of overhead cables to find a stile into a lane. Turn left to cross the River Arrow and return to Pembridge. ●

The River Arrow at Eardisland Bridge

17 *Hergest Ridge*

Kington is a charming, thriving small market town, little affected by modern building and retaining all of the character of bygone days. It stands on Offa's Dyke Path and so is popular with ramblers. This walk rises from the town's church onto the rounded, windy hill of Hergest Ridge, unveiling extraordinary views across the Marches and into Wales. Along the way are a national plant collection and one of the oldest houses in the county.

START Kington town centre (grid ref: SO 296567)

DISTANCE 5¼ miles (8.4km)

TIME 2½ hours

PARKING Main car park (Pay and Display), Mill Street, Kington (next to tourist information centre)

ROUTE FEATURES Largely on back lanes and grassy paths on common land. One long, gradual climb onto Hergest Ridge

From the Market Hall walk up Church Street, past The Swan Hotel and continue to rise out of the town centre. Take the lychgate into St Mary's churchyard and take the opportunity to visit this historic old church. Inside is the fine alabaster effigy tomb of Thomas and Ellen Vaughan. Below the churchyard is a massive old wooded motte, all that remains of the town's short-lived, 12th century castle.

Leave the churchyard by the west entrance and walk to the main road. Carefully cross into Ridgebourne Road, signed for Ridgebourne and Hergest Croft, joining the route of Offa's Dyke Path. Some way up this quiet lane is Hergest Croft. This is set in 50 acres (20ha) of landscaped gardens and is particularly noted for its national collection of maple and birch trees (open April to October). Remain on Ridgebourne Road until it ends at a gateway.

Ⓐ Go through the gate and take the wider of the two tracks, a grassy swathe that gradually rises up Hergest Ridge. An Offa's Dyke

PUBLIC TRANSPORT Buses to Kington from Hereford and Leominster
REFRESHMENTS Plenty of cafés, inns, pubs and shops in Kington
PUBLIC TOILETS Kington
ORDNANCE SURVEY MAPS Explorer 201 (Knighton & Presteigne)

Bradnor Hill from Ridgebourne Road, Kington

Path finger-post soon confirms the route, although it is impossible to miss. Simply continue the easy ascent, your reward being exceptional views to the north. Off to your right, the nearest hill is Bradnor Hill, hosting England and Wales's highest golf course reaching to nearly 1300ft (396m). Beyond this is the shapely Herrock Hill and then serried folds and ridges leaping north towards Knighton. Farther west are Black Mixen (with a radio mast) and the upwellings of Radnor Forest, glorious unspoilt uplands of sheep walks, moors and deep valleys.

About 300 yds (274m) past a memorial bench you'll reach a major crossing of paths, just before a low waymark post. At this major crossing turn left (not sharp left) along a wide grassy path through the bracken. This shortly starts a long, gradual curve around to the right. Here you lose the views north but gain an incredible panorama stretching across Herefordshire to the looming Black Mountains and Brecon Beacons, the distant smudges of the Malverns and countless other hills.

? *What does the clock tower on Kington Market Hall celebrate?*

The Vaughans were a powerful family who lived at Hergest Court. Thomas 'Black' Vaughan fought and died at the Battle of Banbury in 1469; his widow Ellen became known as Gethin The Terrible after extracting a bloody revenge on her brother's murderer. Hergest Court is where one of Welsh literature's most important medieval books was preserved; *The Red Book of Hergest* is the basis for much lore and legend. The Court is said to be haunted by a demonic hound, the basis for Conan Doyle's *Hound of the Baskervilles*.

B In 300 yds (274m) take a wide path departing sharp left, heading towards a stand of woodland and an isolated farm. Near the corner of the woods a finger-post points the way right of the trees to a farm lane. Now simply remain with this, leaving Hergest Ridge behind to follow the course of a deepening valley down towards the River Arrow. Keep left at a triangular junction (note the castle mound, left) to fall to a T-junction. The farm complex ahead surrounds medieval Hergest Court.

C Turn right, cross the bridge and turn left along the narrow lane. Just past a cottage, right, called Toad Hall, look left for steps up to a stile into pasture. Head slightly

The Vaughan Tomb, St Mary's Church, Kington

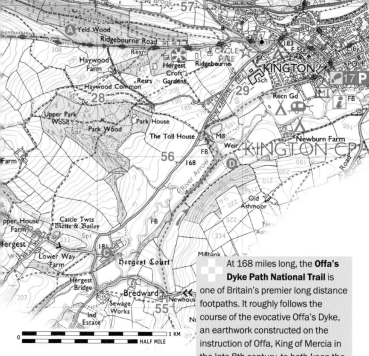

left along the obvious ridge, looking for an open gateway towards the bottom of the hedge line (not the stile below the woods) on your right. A cattle path winds through long pastures, trees on your left and Kington's church spire ahead. Ignore the first gate left and go ahead to one with a stile beside it. Keep ahead along a line of oaks, soon passing through a line of trees across the field.

D In 150 yds (137m) look for a waymarked stile, left, drop to the path and keep left to a footbridge.

At 168 miles long, the **Offa's Dyke Path National Trail** is one of Britain's premier long distance footpaths. It roughly follows the course of the evocative Offa's Dyke, an earthwork constructed on the instruction of Offa, King of Mercia in the late 8th century, to both keep the warlike Welsh at bay and act as a barrier to allow tolls and trade fees to be collected. It stretched all the way from Prestatyn in the north to Sedbury (Chepstow) in the south.

Cross this and jink right, then left to another footbridge, go ahead up the narrow copse and then skirt a garden to reach a lane. Turn right, immediately taking the finger-posted path at Tattymoor. From the end of this path, a line of kissing-gates leads to the edge of playing fields. Walk ahead to the lodge house, from where a tarred path leads to the town centre. ●

18 *Craswall*

START Craswall
(grid ref: SO 278360)

DISTANCE 5¼ miles
(8.4km)

TIME 3 hours

PARKING The Bull's Head,
Craswall. Limited
roadside parking here

ROUTE FEATURES Field
paths; farm tracks; back
lanes; moorland paths.
Some gates are difficult
to open

This walk undulates below the flank of Black Hill, the most north-easterly ridge of the Black Mountains that here forms the boundary between England and Wales and where Bruce Chatwin based his touching novel On the Black Hill. *It's an area of remote hill farms, isolated churches and hamlets amidst spectacular scenery, of which this route makes the most, tracing drovers' roads to offer excellent views deep into Mid Wales and across to the Cotswold Hills.*

A steep lane falls to the left of the Bull's Head; take this and drop to the bridge across the infant River Monnow, here starting its tranquil route to join the River Wye at Monmouth. Rise beyond the bridge to a bend, where a gate allows access to the churchyard.

St Mary's Church dates back nearly 800 years and is typical of such places of worship strung through the Black Mountains. Remote and serving a scattered farming community, drovers also

worshipped at such places. They may also have played here; in the north west of the churchyard a depression is recorded as having been a cock-fighting pit whilst a fives court once existed against the northern wall (below the weatherboarded bell turret).

Look for the slab-stile beside a kissing-gate in the north west corner of the churchyard (beneath a fir tree), take this and turn right along the track. Almost immediately, turn left along a track waymarked

PUBLIC TRANSPORT None

REFRESHMENTS The Bull's Head, Craswall

PUBLIC TOILETS None

ORDNANCE SURVEY MAPS Explorer OL13 (Brecon Beacons National Park –
Eastern area)

as the Monnow Valley Walk (MVW) across a cattle-grid. Pass by the barn, step over a stream and take a gate, then a further (rusty) one,

soon heading for the left of the stand of fir trees and another gate into a hedged/fenced track above the woods. Take a further two gates and look right for a new fence and gate. Take this and cross the shallow ford. Go beyond to another gate and ford, then walk ahead up the marshy hollow to the foot of a pasture.

Your target is a gate at the far top corner. Beyond this, stick to the top of the steep field. Down to the left are a few ponds, whilst the horizon is the slopes of Hay Bluff. A corner gate leads to a stretch across bedrock and around to a gateway into the foot of a farmyard.

Ⓐ Turn left down the access road,

Hay Bluff from above Craswall Priory

Stream below Llech y Llandron, Hay Bluff

dropping to a complex of barns. On your left here, a gate allows access to the ruins of Craswall Priory.

Follow the farm lane up to a road and turn left. In about 400 yds

Some monks sought remote sites at which to build their priories. This one was founded by the **French House of Grandmont** and is one of only three in Britain established by this sect. It was sponsored by the local lord of the manor, Walter de Lacy and built in the 1220s. *The remains are in a precarious state, so exercise care.* A faded interpretive board tells you what's what here. The ponds seen earlier are on the site of the original monastic fishponds. The Priory was suppressed in 1462.

(366m), as the lane bends left, take the bridleway through a gate on your right and walk alongside the hedge/fence. As this bends away left, continue ahead across the corner of the field to a gateway on the near horizon. From this keep ahead left to crest the low ridge, from where a series of waymarked gates takes you towards the right of the lone farm.

The views from here are extraordinary. In the valley ahead is Hay-on-Wye, beyond which the Begwn Hills rise, whilst farther north is the line of Radnor Forest beyond Hergest Ridge.

B You'll reach a gate onto the rough lane leading into the grounds of Coed Major Farm. Look to the right for waymarks indicating a track along the edge of the rough terrain and to the right side of the fir plantation. At the far end, go through the waymarked (MVW) gateway and ahead for a short distance. Look left for a worn tractor road; this climbs through reedy upland pasture to meet a more obvious crossing

? What is the unique name of the huge, home-made sandwiches that are a popular meal at the Bull's Head?

fords bring you to the top end of a tarred lane. Join this to return to the Bull's Head. ●

track, along which turn left. The huge views now are eastwards across Herefordshire to the Cotswolds and the Malverns. The track plots a course above the woods, eventually falling to a corner where a stream flows across bare sandstone bedrock.

Cross this to find a gate, continuing beyond along an old sunken track. Several further gates and shallow

St Mary's Church, Craswall

19 *Marcle Ridge*

START Marcle Ridge
(grid ref: SO 630346)
DISTANCE 5½ miles
(8.8km)
TIME 3 hours
PARKING Marcle Ridge
car park. From the A449
in Much Marcle turn for
Woolhope opposite The
Walwyn Arms. Pass the
cider works and then
follow brown signs to the
car park
ROUTE FEATURES Field
paths; farm lanes; back
roads. Several climbs
and descents

Close to the Gloucestershire border, Marcle Ridge rises high above the wide Vale of Leadon, home to some of Herefordshire's finest cider orchards. This walk takes full advantage of the extensive views across to the Malvern and Cotswold Hills before plunging down into the secluded, wooded countryside of the Woolhope Dome to visit the purported home of Dick Whittington, the famous Mayor of London.

Just above the car park look right for steps up to a stile. Fade right beyond this and follow the field edge path along the spine of Marcle Ridge.

The vast transmitter mast dominates, but look east for the reward of the huge panorama across eastern Herefordshire and Gloucestershire. Ledbury nestles at the foot of Frith Hill, beyond which rise the Malverns. Farther south, the horizon is the line of the Cotswolds, eventually disappearing behind the plateau of the Forest of Dean and the distinctive May Hill, capped with 100 trees planted in 1897 to celebrate Queen Victoria's diamond jubilee.

A series of stiles and gates takes the walk to and through the pasture hosting the mast. Further gates bring you to steps and a stile into a rough old lane; turn right down this. Through the gateway ahead, views stretch to the folded hills above the Wye Gorge, whilst far to the west are the Black Mountains.

Remain on this medieval lane, the

PUBLIC TRANSPORT Infrequent buses from Hereford to Woolhope
REFRESHMENTS Pubs in Woolhope
PUBLIC TOILETS None
ORDNANCE SURVEY MAPS Explorer 189 (Hereford & Ross-on-Wye)

Stone Road, to and past an isolated barn, then skirt the foot of woods to reach a tarred lane. Bear right, cross the brook and rise gently for about 250 yds (228m) to find a finger-post and stile, right. An obvious path cuts across fields and below traditional orchards towards the distant barn, joining a lane near fishponds at this idyllic setting.

Ⓐ Look left of the barn for a

waymarked stile into a muddy corner. Stay towards the lower end of this sloping pasture to a stile at an offset corner. Climb this and walk along the foot of the orchard to the farmyard. A waymark at a stile points to a kissing-gate in the fence a short distance in front of the glorious, half-timbered Court Farm here at Sollers Hope. Walk ahead into the churchyard.

> The Saxons built a church here 1300 years ago, although today's St Michael's was founded in AD1390 by Robert Whittington. He was the elder brother of **Dick Whittington**, mayor of London in the early 15th century and one of the richest men in the kingdom. The flat topped mound in the churchyard was a stronghold of the Whittington family, and it is possible that Dick was born here whilst his father was ostracised from the court of Edward III.

> **?** *In which year was Dick Whittington born?*

Ⓑ Near the tower, a gate leads into a pasture. Go half right to a waymarked gate, then keep to the left beside a stream to take two stiles through a horse paddock. Head for a stile right of a brick hut and walk ahead along the upper edge of the long field. The well

Court Farm, Sollers Hope

The Woolhope Dome near Sollers Hope

Herefordshire is renowned for its **cider and orchards;** over 60% of all cider produced in Britain is made in the county. Recent developments have seen dwarf apple tree plantations replace the traditional orchards as these are easier to harvest. In this area, however, the old orchards remain king; those passed on this walk are redolent of days long gone when every farm had its cider mill, and wages were partly paid in cider. A visit to **Weston's Cider Mill** in Much Marcle is highly recommended.

waymarked path passes a neck of woods to cross a footbridge, then continues up a slope to crest a rise, revealing distant Woolhope village.

Cross the next stile and turn left to cross a footbridge in the trees. Keep ahead 50 paces to climb a stile on the right; then head for the cottage half left. Join the rough lane here at Alford's Mill and walk past the house to a left bend. Enter the field on the right here and, as the hedge bends away, keep ahead, well left of the oak, to stiles either side of a lane. Bear right in the field to cross a footbridge, walk up to the corner stile beyond and head for the long dead trees on the low ridge. Beyond these join a lane at a corner and walk ahead to Woolhope.

C The church and Crown Inn are off to the left. To return to the car park turn sharp right for Putley and Ledbury. Stay on this road to reach the Butcher's Arms. Turn right immediately before this and trace this lane round to a fork; keep right on the grass-centred

lane. This roughens and swings
right, passing above a cottage to
reach a gateway.

Follow the fieldside track; then go
ahead to the waymarked stile at the
edge of woods. Drop along the

path within the woods to enter an
enormous field at the head of the
secluded Hyde Valley. Keep the
hedge on your left to rise to a
corner and a hedged track climbing
up to a lane. Turn right to return to
the car park.

●

20 *Coppet Hill*

START Goodrich
(grid ref: SO 575196)
DISTANCE 5½ miles
(8.8km)
TIME 3 hours
PARKING Goodrich Castle
car park
ROUTE FEATURES Lanes;
woodland paths;
riverside paths

*A visit to one of the Marches' favourite
castles is the culmination of this walk. An
initially steep climb on to Coppet Hill is
rewarded with tremendous views, whilst a
stretch of riverside path follows the Wye as
it prepares to enter its renowned gorge below the
sentinel of the famous Yat Rock. This is a good wildlife
walk, with fallow deer, buzzard, various woodpeckers
and orchids regularly seen; look out, too, for
cormorants on the River Wye.*

Walk down the car park
approach road to the junction in
Goodrich. Turn sharp left here,
joining the 'No Through Road'
signed for Welsh Bicknor and
Courtfield. This rises gradually to
reach a triangular junction at a
small green. Look directly behind
this for a noticeboard naming
Coppet Hill Common Local
Nature Reserve and a flight of
steps rising steeply beyond.

Start a long, steady climb here as

several flights of steps wind the
path up through scrub and
undergrowth to emerge into a wide
grassy path amidst bracken and
thorny scrub. The slope lessens as
you approach the triangulation
pillar near the highest point of
Coppet Hill.

Mouthwatering views are unveiled
to most points of the compass. To
the north is distant Titterstone
Clee above Ludlow, capped by a
radar dome; farther west are the

PUBLIC TRANSPORT Buses to Goodrich from Ross-on-Wye and Monmouth
REFRESHMENTS Pub and shop in Goodrich; seasonal snack bar at the car park
PUBLIC TOILETS Car park
ORDNANCE SURVEY MAPS Explorer OL14 (Wye Valley and Forest of Dean)

smudge of the Mortimer Forest and the dark mass of Radnor Forest's moor-topped hills whilst way out west are the Black Mountains, the sharply defined Sugar Loaf and Skirrid hills above Abergavenny and the distinct peaks of the Brecon Beacons.

Near at hand to the west, the Wye starts one of its tight loops. Were the lie of the land slightly kinder, you'd also be able to see the river to the north, east and south as Coppet Hill is essentially a peninsula of quartz conglomerate rock, isolated by the Wye millions of years ago.

Ⓐ Continue along the wide path, passing by a chimney and fallen walls, a site known locally as The Folly. A stand of thick woodland to the left obscures views across to the Forest of Dean plateau. However, as the walk progresses along the ridge, occasional vistas open out through gateways across to the delicate spire of Ruardean's church and the tumbled, wooded hills and sharp valleys that characterise the edge of the forest.

The path soon begins a long, gradual descent off the ridge. Ahead, the sharp eyed may pick out the profile of Yat Rock against the distant trees that clothe the start of the tortuous Wye Gorge. Lower down, the path enters

Goodrich village from Coppet Hill

woodlands of coppiced hazel and old yews, eventually dropping to a woodside stile and a meadow. Walk ahead to the riverbank and turn right, downstream.

B On the opposite bank, hanging woodlands cling precariously to the massive limestone cliffs and buttresses that form Coldwell Rocks including, off to the left, Needle Rock and Ship Rock. The cliffs end abruptly at a lip where the famous Yat Rock viewpoint is located; look for the tiny figures leaning over the wall here.

Some of these rock pinnacles are home, in spring and summer, to

Goodrich Castle

peregrine falcons. You've much more chance, however, of seeing some of Coppet Hill's herd of fallow deer; elusive creatures at the best of times, but which can regularly be seen close to the woodland edge up to your right as the walk progresses along the riverbank.

It's simply a matter of tracing the path through several stiles to arrive at the point where the woods, briefly, fringe the river again.

C At the far end of this wooded arm, go through a field gate and keep beside the trees, walking along to another Coppet Hill Common signboard just a short distance before a barn at Mainoaks

> Surrounded by a precipitous dry moat, **Goodrich Castle** originated about the time of Domesday, built by one Godric Mapplestone to help defend a strategic crossing of the Wye against the Welsh. It matured in the following centuries into one of the most formidable Marcher castles, and continued in use long after many of its contemporaries. It was subject to a siege in the English Civil War, with the Royalist defenders eventually succumbing to a bombardment by a fearsome canon, **Roaring Meg**, in 1646. Colonel John Birch (see Walk 8 Weobley) led this assault and ensured that the castle could never again be used as a powerbase. The castle is open throughout the year.

Farm. Take the stile on the right here, picking up a path through the fringe of the woods and passing above the farmhouse.

This old path follows the course of a mossy wall to eventually emerge from the oak woods above a cottage at the foot of Coppet Hill. Pick up the lane beyond this and walk this past a string of houses and cottages to a tarred lane. Keep left along this to find the triangular junction, go left here and then right at the junction to return to the castle car park. Goodrich Castle itself is a short walk beyond the end of the car park.

? What is the feature known as a garderobe in the castle?

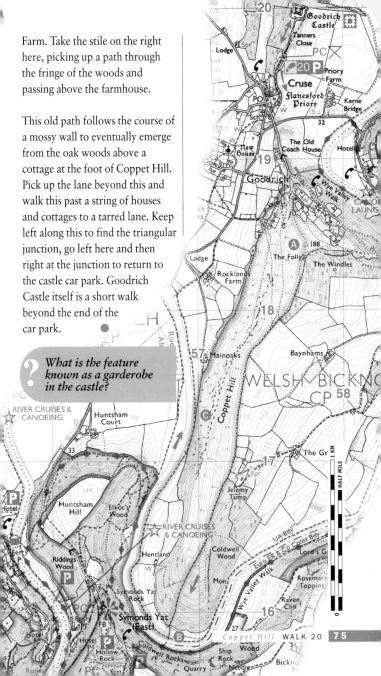

Further Information

Walking Safety

Always take with you both warm and waterproof clothing and sufficient food and drink. Wear suitable footwear such as strong walking boots or shoes that give a good grip over stony ground, on slippery slopes and in muddy conditions. Try to obtain a local weather forecast and bear it in mind before you start. Do not be afraid to abandon your proposed route and return to your starting point in the event of a sudden and unexpected deterioration in the weather.

All the walks described in this book will be safe to do, given due care and respect, even during the winter. Indeed, a crisp, fine winter day often provides perfect walking conditions, with firm ground underfoot and a clarity of light unique to that time of the year.

The most difficult hazard likely to be encountered is mud, especially when walking along woodland and field paths, farm tracks and bridleways – the latter in particular can often get churned up by cyclists and horses. In summer, an additional difficulty may be narrow and overgrown paths, particularly along the edges of cultivated fields. Neither should constitute a major problem provided that the appropriate footwear is worn.

Follow the Country Code

- Enjoy the countryside and respect its life and work
- Guard against all risk of fire
- Take your litter home
- Fasten all gates
- Help to keep all water clean
- Keep your dogs under control
- Protect wildlife, plants and trees
- Keep to public paths across farmland
- Take special care on country roads
- Leave livestock, crops and machinery alone
- Make no unnecessary noise
- Use gates and stiles to cross fences, hedges and walls

(The Countryside Agency)

Useful Organisations

For accomodation, event details and general information about the county go to **www.visitorlinks.com**

Forest Enterprise
Forest of Dean District, Bank House, Bank Street, Coleford, Gloucestershire

Broad Street, Weobley

GL16 8BA
(*including Herefordshire Forestry
Commission woodlands*)
Tel. 01594 833057 or 810983

**Herefordshire Council Parks and
Countryside Service**
PO Box 41, Leominster,
Herefordshire HR6 0ZA
Tel. 01568 798320 or 797052

Malvern Hills AONB
Manor House, Grange Road,
Malvern, Worcestershire
WR14 3EY
Tel. 01684 560616
www.malvernhillsaonb.org.uk

Malvern Hills Conservators
Manor House, Grange Road,
Malvern, Worcestershire
WR14 3EY
Tel. 01684 892002
www.malvernhills.org.uk

National Trust
West Midlands Regional Office,
Attingham Park,
Shrewsbury,
Shropshire SY4 4TP
Tel. 01743 709343
www.nationaltrust.org.uk/regions/
westmidlands

Wye Valley AONB
Hadnock Road, Mayhill,
Monmouth, Monmouthshire
NP25 3NG
Tel. 01600 713977
www.wyevalleyaonb.co.uk

Rights of Way

Any problems with blocked paths and bridleways, damaged stiles and so on in Herefordshire should be reported to:

The Rights of Way Officer,
Herefordshire Council,
PO Box 234, Hereford HR1 2ZB
Tel. 01432 260572

Local Tourist Information Centres

Bromyard
Tel. 01885 482341 (winter)
    01885 482038 (summer)

Hay-on-Wye
Tel. 01497 820144

Hereford
Tel. 01432 268430

Kington
Tel. 01544 230778 (seasonal)

Ledbury
Tel. 01531 636147

Leominster
Tel. 01568 616460

Ross-on-Wye
Tel. 01989 562768

Queenswood
(near Leominster)
Tel. 01568 797842 (seasonal)

Black Hill and Hatterrall Ridge from Longtown Castle

Deer in Eastnor Park

Public Transport

For all enquiries about local bus and train services in Herefordshire ring **Traveline** on:

Tel. 0870 6082608

(Special bus services are provided during the summer in both the Malvern Hills AONB and the Wye Valley AONB. Timetables for both, the *Malvern Hills Hopper* and the *Wye Valley Wanderer* are available from tourist information centres throughout the county).

Ordnance Survey Maps

Explorers

OL12 (Brecon Beacons National Park – Western & Central areas)

OL13 (Brecon Beacons National Park – Eastern area)

OL14 (Wye Valley and Forest of Dean)

189 Hereford & Ross-on-Wye
190 Malvern Hills & Bredon Hill
201 Knighton & Presteigne
202 Leominster & Bromyard
203 Ludlow

Answers to Questions

Walk 1: 1893 (churchyard information board).

Walk 2: St Mary and St David.

Walk 3: It commemorates Captain Reginald Somers-Cox MC who was killed in the First World War, and it marks the gift of the hill and fort to the National Trust in 1923.

Walk 4: King Henry III (church leaflet).

Walk 5: From Clydawg, a 5th-century Welsh prince who was murdered here (church pamphlet).

Walk 6: 236 yards (tee marker).

Walk 7: There are 23 steps up and 33 steps down.

Walk 8: The de Lacy family (castle ring information board).

Walk 9: A maximum of six people.

Walk 10: The spire was erected in 1974 and cost over £30,000.

Walk 11: S7874 (on a metal inset at the base of the pillar).

Walk 12: Richard Boyys was vicar here for 59 years between 1476 – 1535.

Walk 13: It's the old church clock machinery, nearly 500 years old.

Walk 14: The new church of All Saints was built half a mile away in 1841 (chapel information leaflet).

Walk 15: A leaping salmon.

Walk 16: Sweden (bell tower information board).

Walk 17: It celebrates Queen Victoria's diamond jubilee in 1897.

Walk 18: Huffers.

Walk 19: 1358 (information sheets in the church).

Walk 20: It's the name given to a toilet, the waste from which gushed into the dry moat around the castle.

The rope ferry between Symonds Yat East and West